DIARY OF THE ONE SWELLING SEA

DIARY OF THE ONE
SWELLING SEA

Jill McCabe Johnson

MoonPath Press

Poetry
ISBN 978-1-936657-06-3

Author photo by Charles Toxey

Design by Tonya Namura
using Perpetua

MoonPath Press is dedicated to publishing the
best poets of the U.S. Northwest Pacific states

MoonPath Press
PO Box 1808
Kingston, WA 98346

MoonPathPress@yahoo.com

http://MoonPathPress.com

ACKNOWLEDGMENTS

Thank you to the editors of the following journals:
Eudaimonia Poetry Review:
   "Day Dolomite," and "Day Paddle-Tail"
Shark Reef:
   "Day Cyclone," "Day Floor-Fault"
Terrain.org:
   "Day Hinge-Tooth," "Day Precipice," and
   "Day Vesicle"

Thanks to Jonis Agee, Noah Ashenhurst, Grace Bauer, Marvin Bell, Jennifer Brennock, Kevin Clark, Stephen Corey, Jeff Curran, James Engelhardt, Casey Fuller, Linda Henry, Erin Hollowell, David Huddle, Annie Johnson, Doug Johnson, Ingrid Karnikis, Nima Kian, Judith Kitchen, Ted Kooser, JoEllen Moldoff, Michelle Reed, Julie Riddle, Marjorie Rommel, Stan Rubin, Tina Schumann, Michael Schmeltzer, and Dorothy Trogdon for their encouragement and insights.

Thank you to Corinne Duchesne and Garrett Hope for past and future collaborations.

TABLE OF CONTENTS

FOR CHARLES. FOR EVER.

DIARY OF THE ONE
SWELLING SEA

Day Sojourn

I lifted the great logs of driftwood today,
    nudged them an inch or two
        onto the grassy borders,
I don't like touching the Dead Zone,
    but my girth expands more than
        the usual expirations.
                How did I get so big?

Day Flight

When air fish ride my back,
   their weight accentuates
        my outer sway. They rest. They eat.
     Then they spread their feather fins and swim
into Sky as their tails rip wedges of water
      away from me. I don't mind. It doesn't hurt.
        Everything always comes back to me.
My water always falls back.

Day Midnight

Sun hid from me today. Pale Mirror
    got in his way. I'm drawn to Mirror,
  for reasons I cannot fathom
just as I don't know why I echo Sky.
    Sun brings gifts of heat and ascension
      when he lulls my water into vapors.
Then Wind carries me to cool
  the barren betweens. Everything
    in life is giving and returning.
  Even Mirror, my night mistress,
rocks me into her push pull give and take.

Day Cutreef

Most of my lovelies live in the shallows.
    Corals shape the clement lagoons
that trap and enrapture Sun's heat.

Blue starling, sideways crawler, damselfish and spiny.
    Everyone follows plankton,
swallows her into his heart.

But when reef's crusty edges break,
    I can't stop my cooler waves pawling in.
Water goes where water goes.

Day Frigate

Monkey cups slice my surface. They float,
                              but they also churn,
leaving sea ribbons and sun fish
                    streaming in pieces behind.
Sometimes I capsize the cups,
        but their casements and rotting flesh
                    gnaw at my depths. I've learned.
Contaminations can never be contained.
            Better to give the cups passage back,
                              back to their Dead Zone.

Day Flora

Sun does his best
　　　　　　to extract my shadow makers,
but the clouds dissipate
　　　　　　as soon as they form.
　　Night can't cool
　　　　　　my fevered massiveness.
　　Nothing can stop
　　　　　　this orgy of budding,
　as my fringe prods a graveyard
　　　　　　of shells tainted red.

Day Razorbelly

In warmwater
    the kelee shad
        slivers light like waves
   then slides his silverscale
          through brackenmuck,
            snaring diatom and phytos
     in gillraker's open sway.

Day Monster

Hollow bones and drifting teeth
        ride in the center of me.
Pale as my mistress,

but synthetic as sweeper nets—
        I dare not give it a name.
Island of emptiness.

Clump of death. It corrodes
        into cellular venoms
that lodge in my lovelies.

The sea jellies have it worst.
        I wish the monkey cups
        would bear it away.

Day Reckon

They monkey-pierced
my mistress' polar valleys
and she bleeds

what little water she retains.
Her ache is my ache;
higher and higher the waves.

Beware, you monkey frigates.
You cannot guess the bounds of my wrath.
Foam and furor. Flood and rankle.

Turbulent times, these.
Turbulent, turbulent times.

Day Shadowcast

Sun beckoned my shadow makers today.
    They lifted into sky—
        away from tidal chivalries
yet closer to Mirror's face.

My mistress' eyes
    really do shine like Sun,
        they share his luminescence,
his moment, his largesse.

When wind nudges
    my shadow makers to mountains,
        I surrender to the cycle.
Wind aspires and I ascend.

Ever at the call of Mirror.
    Even when helping Sun.
        Ever devoted to Mirror.
Mirror and her mesmeric heart.

Day Dwindle

Barnacles love a slow decay.
        They latch onto the sleepy forever
of disintegration. Rocks, metals, and drifty logs.
      My bubbles help, turning ore iron-red,
and copper plankton-blue,
        like the inside of a cuttlefish
that leaks a flush of seeping twilight
      after the seal assails.

Day Precipice

Sharks launch like fast-floating eggs off the
    cliff bank.
        Face of dark gardens where sea sponge,
          urchin, and cucumber
        lurk along walls. Deep in an eddy of
         ever-night,
            octopus undulates and waits.
    She wraps her arms in tentacled embrace
          to glut on the valiant shark.

Day Memory

In night waves
the stars pinprick to nothingness
the way my surface-skins
flicker Sun's pain.
Echoes surge
in solitary currents where
grief is the wash
of silt at sea bottom,
endless and never swept clean.

Day Fracture

Each day a little more,
Earth cracks open like Sky.
Time reveals fissures
that draw me into fresh openings.
When Earth shakes hard like
mangrove leaves,
she sends me lapping
where brine doesn't belong.
Sun, Mirror, Wind, and Sea.
We are the only constants.

16

Day Rivermouth

Water teems as salmon leap
> over the spilling rush.
   Plump with roe
     and smelling for home,
> the finfish surge into goodbye.
Come summer-shift,
     snowmelt will carry
> the hatchlings to saltiness
   while airfish flutter
     their shadows toward poles.

Day Vesicle

       Ulve-weeds drift in surface shallows,
their stipe and lamina
      wrought like eel and ray.
    Sun-soaking, greening,
          they trail from buoyant berry-sacs
that sway in the burgeoning tide.

Day Paddle-Tail

Half the day in sleepiness, lolling
    up to water's break for sky-breaths,
but barely stirring from her manatee dreams.
    The other half lipping turtle grass
and recalling her newly weaned calf.

Day Dolomite

Sands and salts, oolites and lime
    mingle in the loam sludge sediment
where eel secretes her larvae to hatch.
        Under a floating island of sargassam
  hides a loggerhead turtle
      who hankers for eggs among the crystals,
          yolks of silt and glory

Day Cyclone

Sky eddies swirl like the spinning dolphin
    mad for his lover who watches in awe.
        The tempest froths my surface-skins,
and sprays torrents for Wind to scatter
    into the puckered day.
        Tomorrow calm.
        Tomorrow the drifties.

Day Hinge-Tooth

       Siphons, where the edges fuse,
    milk tiny rivulets of weave-water
in and out of their calcite shells.
             Razors dig and scallops swim.
Like mussels they marry
    the mantle and shell
        coupled in dorsal desire.

Day Fjord

Where ice had ploughed troughs,
 my deepest waters sleep
despite waves rolling over the sill.
 Sea nursery for trout, herring,
and the right-eyed flounder.
Feeding pool for black-tailed godwits,
 breeding for osprey and seal.
Here, only my skin-waters pitch
 in echo to Mirror's heave.
But down in the deepies where flatfish burrow,
 impulse lies fallow as dark.

Day Madrigal

Humpbacks call from the calving grounds.
Melodious flirtations that pulse from melon heads.
Tide after tide, sun after sun,
till the female selects her chanteur.
Grunt, groan, thwop, and snort,
the other whales bark their dissent.

Day Floor-Fault

       Where sea grounds bow skyward,
     waters boil. Dome of heat and stretch,
as rifts and junctions
           budge the wombly crust
    like wrinkles in turtle's neck.
But for every burgeoning, compaction.
       Rock into rock pushing magma
up Mountain's igneous spring.

Day Krill

Swarms mimic coral
ruched in the epitides.
      The swirling flock shimmies
orange filament and rake
     where whale and airfish dine.

Day Filter Feed

Scallops migrate plankton toward their mouths.
    Their cilia siphon errant wanderers
  between fluted husks. The eyes know
motion and Sun's refracted light,
    but cannot distinguish algae, salps, or jellyfish,
from their own miniscule larvae
  that they swallow in hunger and bliss.

Day Sea Nettle

Frills flow between long threads of nerve,
                        and the bell-shaped polyps
            pulse with the knowledge
                        ocelli gather as they sense
        Sky from floor,
                wave from shore.
    The sea nettle stolons
                    strand in connective colonies
                            of floating jelly bloom.

Day Naked-Gill

Sea slugs molt larval shells
    to grant their rush of back gills
ample space to breathe.

After eating anemones,
    they stash the sting-spray
in kleptopockets,
        then harpoon-fire in reflex
            whenever fish sidle near.

Day Tentilla

Stroking, stroking, the comb teeth draggle
      and swim in rhythmic waves.
Tentilla squirt their prey gummy-stuck
         then liquefy him into dinner slurry
    to waft down feeding canals.

Day Blowhole

Vertical sea caves
blast gusts of spray
reaching out to Mirror.
Devotion throbs with patience
beating these limestone walls.
But water will not be pent.
Channels form. Pressure builds.

Day Slack Water

My only rest comes in the lulls
                    of unchanging amplitude
        at the crest of high tide
                or ebb of low:
my only reprieve from Mirror's heave,
                    the only time I feel lost.

Day Adélie

Adélie scamper on floes and fast-ice
    the same wobbly way drifties bob
        when caught across the current.
At rest, the penguins close
    their eyes against cold.
    At conjunction, they stare,
ring-eyed in wonderment.
     Come summer-shift,
        each waits in their nest of stone
    for a turn cozying the egg.

Day Silverfish

Flicking pink and platinum shimmers,
     silverfish tease the penguins and Weddell seal
perched on icy shelves.

The flashfish carry caches of colloidal warm-balm
     as they traverse icy waters.
In death, the wrigglers coalesce
     into shining, sterling floats.

Day Incursion

My surges bulge the way fish bellies swell with roe.
    Driftie logs and edge-dwellers
        flood the monkey boxes and streams.
Their detritus floats coreward
    and I try to send it back, but
             for every whip, a lash.
The tides know their way home.

When Mirror tugs my swell,
       I cannot help but rise to her.
           Every part of me replies.
Crests and crescendos, poundings and peaks.

Day Bounty

Oh, the beautiful plankton
    flourishes under Sun's care.
        Everyone eats well tonight,
    fish and the finless,
        mollusks and me.
  Bask in warmth.
        Bask in simple drift.

Day Oil Spill

Carapaces form on my surface.
  Today's bubbled from beneath,
      shooting blasts of black
        thicker than octopus ink.
Wind and Mirror help me
  slough scraps of the sludge-skin
                  onto the Dead Zone.

I endure,
        but my lovelies, they suffer.

Day Basalt

Vesicular, matrix, or frothy scoria,
        its glassy facets glisten like Sky
as magma emerges with each starview spin.
            Upwelling in heat, cooling in answer—
        the volcanic-chain ritual
                        of simmer and subside.

Day Petal-Back

Its watersides gleam white
        to hide under clouds
                as the loonfish flaps
    feather-fins to air.

      But its skysides flicker light
           off petal-lined plumage
                whenever loon plunges
      for leech and snail.

Day Sea Sponge

Wan pore-bearer,
with its silica spikes,
            can absorb a pure-zing
electrical charge
    without collapsing.
                Sponge basket radiates
    luminescence to the deepies,
and food to the pair
            of mated shrimp
sequestered in its crystal walls.

Day Rotifer

Tufted crown and single foot,
the whirlies inch
   along the substrate,
      toes seeking in grasp and pull,
         till they latch on solid
then cilia-swish
         swift currents of phytos
               into their gaping maws.

Day Burrow

Sand-digger edges
                        its pansy disc shell
to steal through low-water silt.

The underbelly spines
                        slither and ripple
to span soft-bottom beds.

Day Sea Urchin

Sea floor's brittle star
    tastes changes in water like sunlight
                    and falling beech pollen
        swept in current's stream.

Day Shiver-Skate

Slivered beneath sand
the stingray's eyes and tail
breech while he eats.

When he skimmers after his mate,
he nips her disc like a seal pup

then claspers her valve
to surge into her yolk-sac
where babies squirm and skate.

Day Cephalon

Murking in the slush
of intertidal silt
his eyes have surrendered
clarity and color,
but detritus glides
into grinding hungers
like seaweed
minced in the grist.

Day Thermal

Wings stiff in glide,
        pelicans stream after pelicans
                riding Wind's crest.
They soar to feeding spaces,
        herding shad, menhaden and
                herring into surface shallows
        to sweep, scoop and swallow.

Day Foreshore

Inundation bears down on the limpets
    swept and draped like sea lettuce on rocks.
The swash zone wears the weal,
      pounding after pounding, bearing the brunt
        of Mirror's insatiable tide.

Day Ossicle

Sea star's tube feet and pom-pom tufts
        grab and kill krill.
But to eat mussels, he pries the bivalve casings
    then thrusts his feeder past broken dreams
        where tenderness resides.

Day Sea Floor

Solitary isopod scours the jetsam
                    that litters clay bottom floors.
        Plodding, she shreds cucumber,
                    sponge, and the fallen cadavers
of fish, squid, and whale.
                        When finflicks approach,
                she twines her segments
            into stony, plated foil.

Day Manca

Eggs float in marsupial reverie
till the tots crawl
out of their womb-pockets.
Sightless crustaceans,
they muster and lean
all of their yearning toward heat.

Day Milky Way

Star scatter stretches above me.
I watch when blue sleeps.
Milky Way is the master of expansion.
But lately when I stretch, I don't fully recede.
Milky Way shows me
the inescapable sureness
of expand and expire.
Still I maintain my evermore habits,
rocking and rising, falling and foam.

ABOUT THE AUTHOR

Jill McCabe Johnson is the editor of the anthologies *Becoming: What Makes a Woman* (2012) and *Being: What Makes a Man* (2013) from the University of Nebraska Gender Programs. She is the recipient of the Editor's Prize in Poetry from *ScissorTale Review*, the Paula Jones Gardiner Award from Floating Bridge Press, and has received Pushcart Prize nominations for her poetry, fiction, and nonfiction. Her writing can be found in a wide range of journals, including *Brevity, Compass Rose, The Los Angeles Review, terrain.org, Iron Horse Literary Review, Umbrella*, and *Harpur Palate*.

Jill is the founder and executive director of Artsmith, a non-profit to support the arts. She earned her MFA at the Rainier Writing Workshop at Pacific Lutheran University, and is pursuing a PhD in English at the University of Nebraska—Lincoln. Jill and her husband enjoy exploring the woods and waters of their home in the San Juan Islands archipelago.

Made in the USA
San Bernardino, CA
01 September 2014